BLESSED NAMES
Why Was He Named ar-Ridha (A)?
Written by:
Kisa Kids Publications

Please recite a Fātiḥah for the marḥūmīn
of the Rangwala family, the sponsors of this book.

All proceeds from the sale of this book
will be used to produce more educational resources.

Dedication
This book is dedicated to the beloved Imām of our time (AJ). May Allāh (swt) hasten his reappearance and help us to become his true companions.

Acknowledgements
Prophet Muḥammad (s): The pen of a writer is mightier than the blood of a martyr.

True reward lies with Allāh, but we would like to sincerely thank Shaykh Salim Yusufali and Sisters Sabika Mithani, Liliana Villalvazo, Zahra Sabur, Kisae Nazar, Sarah Assaf, Nadia Dossani, Fatima Hussain, Naseem Rangwala, and Zehra Abbas. We would especially like to thank Nainava Publications for their contributions. May Allāh bless them in this world and the next.

Preface
Prophet Muḥammad (s): Nurture and raise your children in the best way. Raise them with the love of the Prophets and the Ahl al-Bayt (a).

Literature is an influential form of media that often shapes the thoughts and views of an entire generation. Therefore, in order to establish an Islamic foundation for the future generations, there is a dire need for compelling Islamic literature. Over the past several years, this need has become increasingly prevalent throughout Islamic centers and schools everywhere. Due to the growing dissonance between parents, children, society, and the teachings of Islām and the Ahl al-Bayt (a), this need has become even more pressing. Al-Kisa Foundation, along with its subsidiary, Kisa Kids Publications, was conceived in an effort to help bridge this gap with the guidance of ʿulamah and the help of educators. We would like to make this a communal effort and platform. Therefore, we sincerely welcome constructive feedback and help in any capacity.

The goal of the *Blessed Names* series is to help children form a lasting bond with the 14 Māʿṣūmīn by learning about and connecting with their names. We hope that you and your children enjoy these books and use them as a means to achieve this goal, inshāʾAllāh. We pray to Allāh to give us the strength and tawfīq to perform our duties and responsibilities.

With Duʾās,
Nabi R. Mir (Abidi)

Disclaimer: Religious texts have not been translated verbatim so as to meet the developmental and comprehension needs of children.
Copyright © 2017; 2019 by Al-Kisa Foundation; SABA Global

All rights reserved. First edition 2017. Second edition 2019. No part of this publication may be reproduced, distributed, or transmitted in any form or by any means, including photocopying, recording, or other electronic or mechanical methods, without the prior written permission of the publisher, except in the case of brief quotations embodied in critical reviews and certain other noncommercial uses permitted by copyright law. For permission requests, please write to the publisher at the address below.

Kisa Kids Publications
4415 Fortran Court
San Jose, CA 95134
(260) KISA-KID [547-2543]

An Introduction to the Blessed Names

Our names are a very special part of us. Many times, they shape our personalities and even explain who we are or the person we would like to become. In this series, you will explore the names and titles of our beloved 14 Ma'soomeen. Did you know that their names and titles were not just ordinary names? They were special because they were given to them by Allah!

Allah has given seven special heavenly names to our Ma'soomeen: Muhammad, Ali, Fatimah, Hasan, Husain, Ja'far, and Musa. Behind each of these names is a heavenly power!

In addition to their names, each of the Ma'soomeen also had special titles by which they became famous. Their titles were often given to them because of the circumstances of their time, but these titles and characteristics were common amongst all the Ma'soomeen. For example, Imam al-Baqir (a) was known for spreading knowledge because he was able to create many new universities and branches of knowledge during his time. However, if the other Ma'soomeen had the same opportunity, they, too, would have spread knowledge and created universities in their teaching circles. In these stories, you will discover some of the reasons why the Ma'soomeen received their specific names or titles.

Many of us share our names with these beloved Ma'soomeen or know people who do. Let's learn about these blessed names and titles so we can strive to be like our blessed Ma'soomeen!

I think ar-Ridha means...

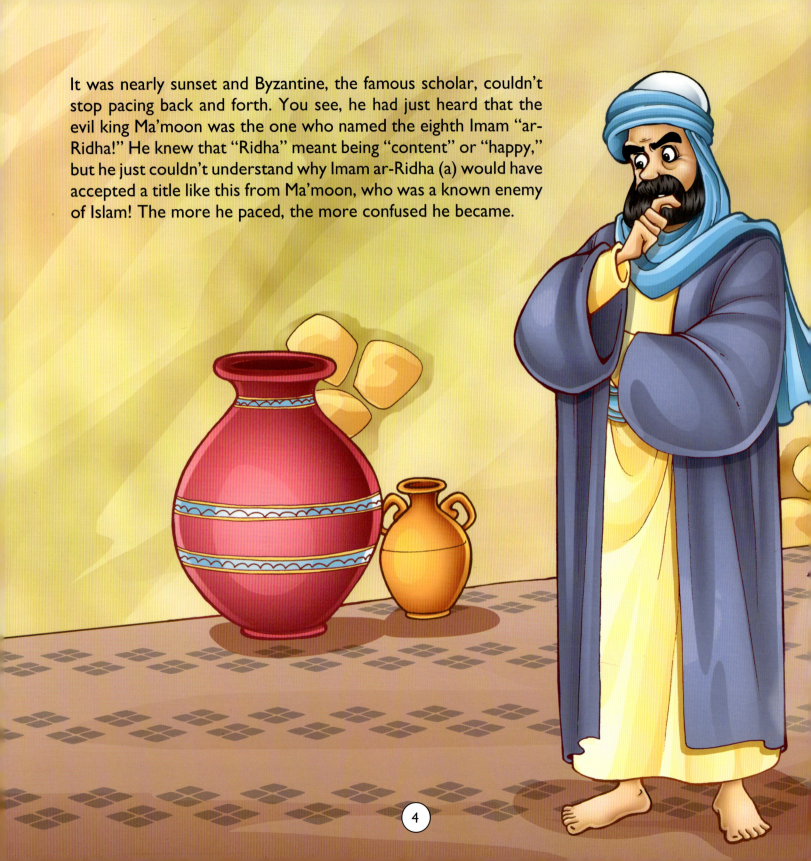

It was nearly sunset and Byzantine, the famous scholar, couldn't stop pacing back and forth. You see, he had just heard that the evil king Ma'moon was the one who named the eighth Imam "ar-Ridha!" He knew that "Ridha" meant being "content" or "happy," but he just couldn't understand why Imam ar-Ridha (a) would have accepted a title like this from Ma'moon, who was a known enemy of Islam! The more he paced, the more confused he became.

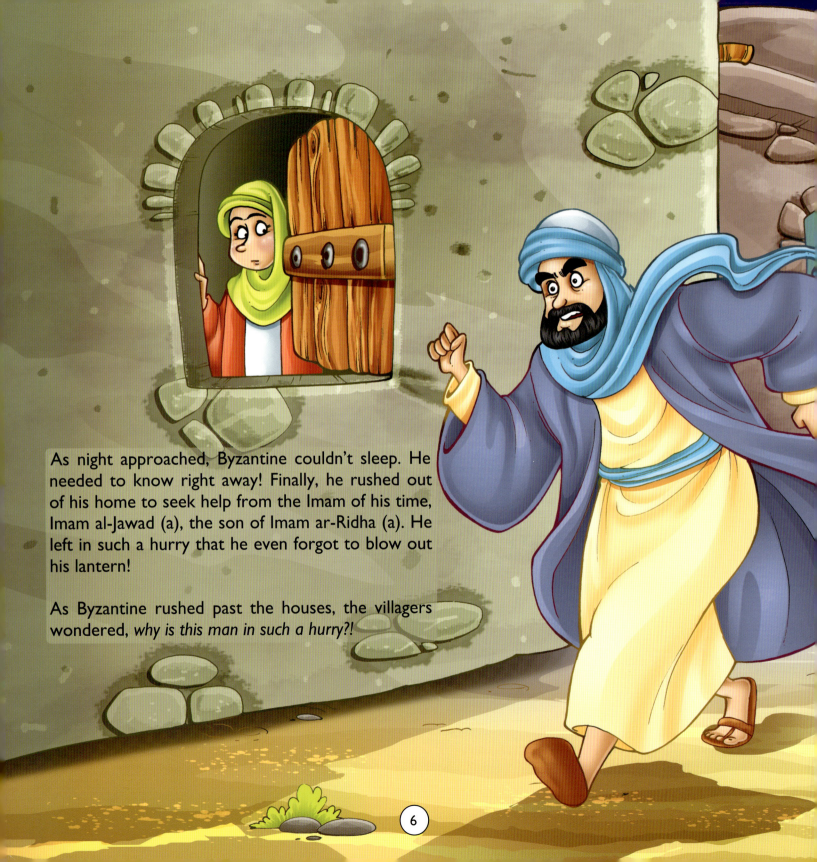

As night approached, Byzantine couldn't sleep. He needed to know right away! Finally, he rushed out of his home to seek help from the Imam of his time, Imam al-Jawad (a), the son of Imam ar-Ridha (a). He left in such a hurry that he even forgot to blow out his lantern!

As Byzantine rushed past the houses, the villagers wondered, *why is this man in such a hurry?!*

When he finally reached the home of Imam al-Jawad (a), he paused before knocking. He thought the Imam (a) might be resting, and he didn't want to disturb him. After going back and forth in his mind, he decided his question was too pressing, and so he gently knocked on the door.

To his delight, Imam al-Jawad (a) happily opened the door. Byzantine asked for permission to enter, and the Imam (a) kindly welcomed him in.

While catching his breath, Byzantine exclaimed, "It has been a long time since a question has bothered me so much! The more I think about it, the more confused I become! May I please ask you my question?" The Imam (a) kindly agreed.

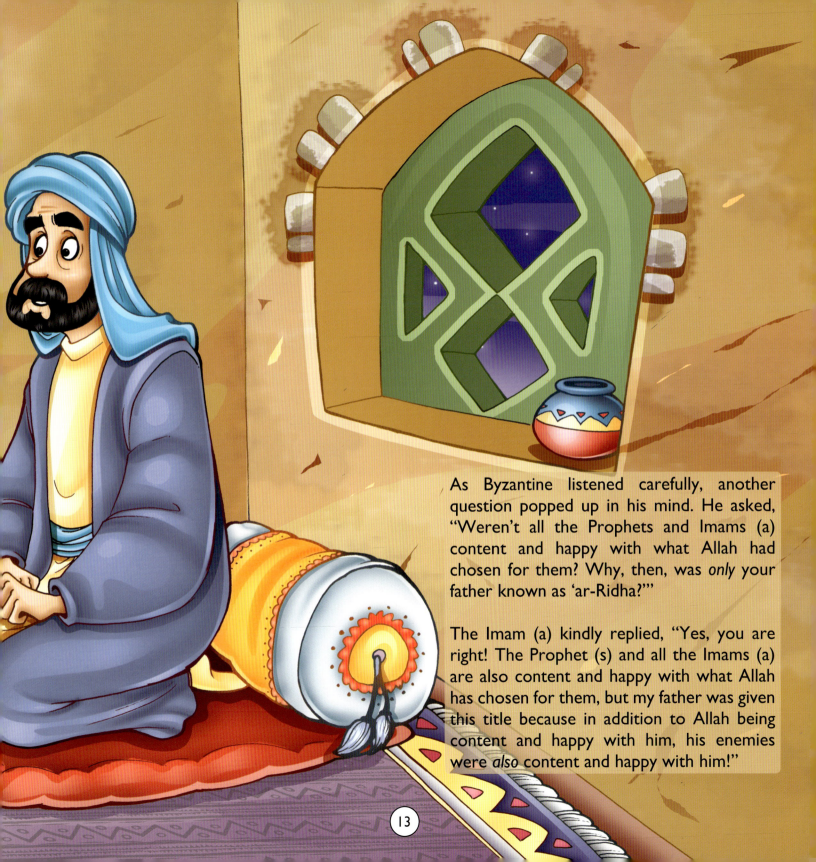

As Byzantine listened carefully, another question popped up in his mind. He asked, "Weren't all the Prophets and Imams (a) content and happy with what Allah had chosen for them? Why, then, was *only* your father known as 'ar-Ridha?'"

The Imam (a) kindly replied, "Yes, you are right! The Prophet (s) and all the Imams (a) are also content and happy with what Allah has chosen for them, but my father was given this title because in addition to Allah being content and happy with him, his enemies were *also* content and happy with him!"

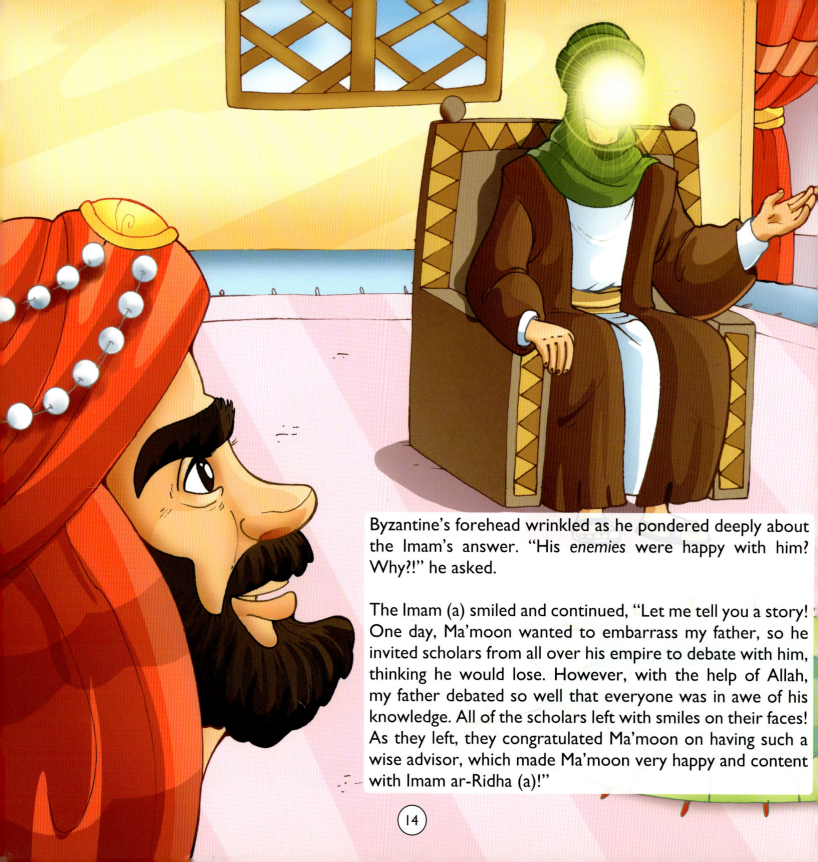

Byzantine's forehead wrinkled as he pondered deeply about the Imam's answer. "His *enemies* were happy with him? Why?!" he asked.

The Imam (a) smiled and continued, "Let me tell you a story! One day, Ma'moon wanted to embarrass my father, so he invited scholars from all over his empire to debate with him, thinking he would lose. However, with the help of Allah, my father debated so well that everyone was in awe of his knowledge. All of the scholars left with smiles on their faces! As they left, they congratulated Ma'moon on having such a wise advisor, which made Ma'moon very happy and content with Imam ar-Ridha (a)!"

Byzantine nodded in approval and breathed a sigh of relief. He had finally received the answer to the question that was driving him crazy with curiosity.

He asked the Imam (a) for permission to leave and bid a happy farewell. He bowed and kissed the Imam's hand out of respect and gratitude, and then excitedly walked back home.

As he made his way home, the sky was completely dark, and the stars twinkled brightly. Nightfall had brought with it fresh, cool air and a sense of peace.

When he walked into his home, he noticed that his lantern was still burning. With a peaceful mind and happy heart, he blew out the lantern and, inspired by Imam ar-Ridha (a), went to sleep feeling content.

O Allah, send your peace and blessings on Imam Ali ar-Ridha (a), who was always pleased with You, and with whom You were always pleased as well.

ʿIlal ash-Sharāiʿ, Vol. 2, P. 237